GOLD

A TRUE BOOK®

by
Salvatore Tocci

Children's Press®
A Division of Scholastic Inc.

New York Toronto London Auckland Sydney
Mexico City New Delhi Hong Kong
Danbury, Connecticut

These coins are made of gold.

Reading Consultant
Julia McKenzie Munemo, MEd
New York, New York

Science Consultant
John A. Benner
Austin, Texas

The photo on the cover shows gold bars. The photo on the title page shows gold rings.

The author and the publisher are not responsible for injuries or accidents that occur during or from any experiments. Experiments should be conducted in the presence of or with the help of an adult. Any instructions of the experiments that require the use of sharp, hot, or other unsafe items should be conducted by or with the help of an adult.

Library of Congress Cataloging-in-Publication Data

Tocci, Salvatore.
   Gold / by Salvatore Tocci.
   p. cm. — (A true book)
   Includes bibliographical references and index.
   ISBN 0-516-23694-6 (lib. bdg.)   0-516-25570-3 (pbk.)
   1. Gold—Juvenile literature. I. Title. II. Series.
QD181.A9T63 2005
669'.22—dc22
                                               2004013147

CHILDREN'S PRESS, and A TRUE BOOK™, and associated logos are trademarks and or registered trademarks of Scholastic Library Publishing.
SCHOLASTIC and associated logos are trademarks and or registered trademarks of Scholastic Inc.
1 2 3 4 5 6 7 8 9 10 R 14 13 12 11 10 09 08 07 06 05

Contents

Lead

Load

Goad

Gold

By changing only one letter at a time, *lead* can be changed into *gold*.

What's Your Favorite Word Game?

Do you like to play word games? Perhaps you enjoy doing word searches or crossword puzzles. You may have even tried playing a word game that involves changing one word into another word by replacing one letter at a time. For example, can you change *lead* into *gold*? First, change *e* to *o* so that *lead* becomes *load*. Then, change *l* to *g* so that *load* becomes *goad*. Finally, change *a* to *l* so that *goad* becomes *gold*. In just three short steps, you have changed *lead* into *gold*.

Changing lead into gold is something many people have tried to do. However,

Pure gold is much more valuable than pure lead.

these people were not playing a word game. They were trying to change one metal into another. The practice of trying to change lead into gold became known as **alchemy**. The birthplace of alchemy was ancient Egypt. From there, alchemy spread to other parts of the world, including China, Arabia, and Europe.

Those who practiced alchemy in Europe can be divided

into two groups. One group focused on discovering how substances were actually made in nature. Their work led to what is now the science of chemistry. The other group continued to look for ways of changing lead into gold. Their work led to failure. Perhaps they did not know as much about gold as you will after reading this book.

What Is Gold?

Gold is an element. An **element** is the building block of matter. **Matter** is the stuff or material that makes up everything in the universe. This book, the chair you are sitting on, and even you are made of matter.

There are millions of different kinds of matter. However, there are just a few more than one hundred different elements. How can so many different kinds of matter be made up of so few elements? Think about the English language. Just twenty-six letters can be arranged to make up all the words in the English language. Likewise, the one hundred or so elements can

Gold is stored by the U.S. government as solid bars. Each bar weighs almost 28 pounds (13 kilograms).

be arranged to make up all the kinds of matter in the universe.

Every element has a name and a symbol. The symbol for gold is Au. This symbol comes from the Latin word *aurum,* the word the early Romans used for gold. The early Romans, however, were not the first people to admire gold. Before them, the ancient Egyptians wore jewelry made of gold. The gold used to make this jewelry, though, was not pure.

The Romans were the first to develop a method for obtaining pure gold from the ores they took out of the ground and the mountains. Most of this gold was obtained from lands they conquered. The gold was then sent back to Rome to be stored in the government's treasury. The Romans used this gold to make jewelry and coins.

The ancient Romans used gold coins such as this one to buy goods.

Gold, like most other elements, is a metal. One feature that all metals share is their ability to conduct electricity. Gold is a good **conductor** of electricity. Unlike most metals, however, pure gold is rather soft. Its softness explains why gold is very **malleable**, which means it can be hammered into many shapes without breaking. It is also **ductile**, which means it can be pressed into a thin sheet or drawn into a wire. Just 1 ounce (28 grams) of pure gold can be hammered until it forms a sheet that measures 30 feet by 10 feet (9 meters by 3 m). In fact, gold is the most ductile metal. Gold is also one of the most expensive metals.

Conducting Electricity

Fold two pieces of aluminum foil several times to make two strips, each about 6 inches (15 centimeters) long and 0.5 inch (1 cm) wide. Tape one end of one foil strip to the negative end of a D-size battery. Wrap the free end of the foil around a gold ring. Wrap one end of the other foil strip around the ring. Be sure that the foil strips do not touch.

Hold the metal base of a flashlight bulb against the positive end of the battery. Touch the free end of the foil strip to the metal ring above the base of the bulb. The bulb should light up. The battery produces electricity that flows through the foil and the gold ring, and lights up the bulb.

Why Is Gold So Expensive?

Gold is expensive for several reasons. First, the world's supply of gold is limited. All the gold that has ever been mined from Earth would fill a container that measures only 55 feet high by 55 feet wide by 55 feet long (18 m by 18 m by 18 m).

All the gold that has ever been mined would fit into about seven of these shipping containers.

All this gold has been collected from every part of the world. Gold can be found in every type of environment, including mountains and river valleys. Gold can even be found in very tiny amounts in seawater.

The largest gold deposit is in South Africa, which has mined about 45 percent of the world's total production of gold. European settlers first discovered gold in South Africa in

1886. That year, they founded the city of Johannesburg. By 1900, some 100,000 Europeans were living in Johannesburg, most of them searching for gold.

The United States experienced a similar reaction to the discovery of gold. In 1848, James Marshall was part of a crew building a sawmill near Sacramento, California. One morning, he discovered a few tiny gold nuggets. Within a few years, nearly 500,000 people from all over the world rushed to California to search for gold and try to become rich. Most of them failed.

California's gold rush ended by 1864. All the gold that could be found in rivers and streams had been removed. Most of the gold still to be discovered was located in rocks deep inside mountains or underground. Only companies with enough money to

People known as prospectors used pans with screens in them to filter the gravel in river and stream bottoms for gold.

hire hundreds of workers and buy expensive machinery were able to go after this gold.

Inside rocks, gold is often mixed with other metals, such as silver, copper, and iron. When gold is mixed with other elements, it is called impure gold. While pure gold has a yellow color, impure gold can be silver-white, orange-red, or even green. People searching for gold are often fooled by its color.

This substance is called "fool's gold" because the yellow specks fool people into thinking it is real gold. Actually, it is a mineral called chalcopyrite.

Yellow specks inside a rock are not always a sign of gold. The first step to finding gold is identifying a spot where it is likely to be found. This step involves taking and analyzing samples. If a sample does contain gold, the next step is figuring out if there is enough gold to make it worthwhile to start digging. A large tunnel may have to be dug deep into a mountain, or a huge mine may have to be dug deep into Earth. The largest gold mine in the United States is about 8,000 feet (2,400 m) beneath the surface. Even when a deposit is found, the gold must be separated from the other elements that are also in the rock. This process is also very expensive.

Gold is difficult to find. Separating gold from other elements is a costly process. These factors are some of the reasons why gold is so valuable. But despite the fact that gold is so expensive, people have always wanted gold for a variety of uses.

How Is Gold Used?

Since ancient times, people have used gold to make jewelry. In 1922, the tomb of Tutankhamen, a young pharaoh who ruled Egypt almost 3,500 years ago, was discovered. Among the items recovered were many pieces of gold jewelry.

This solid gold mask was used to cover the face of King Tutankhamen in his tomb.

Because gold does not corrode, the jewelry was as shiny as it was when the king wore it.

Today, more than one-third of the gold that is mined is used to make jewelry, mostly rings and necklaces. The cost of this jewelry depends partly on the purity of the gold used to make it. The purity of gold is stated in terms of **karats**. Pure gold is said to be 24-karat. However, jewelry made of 24-karat gold can be very soft and may break.

Other metals, such as silver and copper, are mixed with gold to make it stronger. Mixing two or more metals makes an **alloy**.

The metal used to make most gold jewelry is a 14-karat alloy. This means the jewelry is fourteen parts gold and ten parts other metals. Jewelry can also be gold-plated. This type of jewelry is made of another metal, such as copper, that is then covered with a thin layer of a gold alloy.

Preventing Corrosion

Gold is also used in paints. Cover an iron nail with gold leaf paint and place it in a glass jar. Place another iron nail that is not covered with gold leaf paint in a separate glass jar. Cover both nails with white vinegar. Watch what happens to both nails over the next several days.

The iron nail should start to corrode. However, the gold leaf paint should protect the other nail from corrosion. Experiment with juice, soda, and milk to see if they work the same way as white vinegar does.

Gold wires, each thinner than a human hair, are used as conductors in circuit boards.

In addition to jewelry, gold is also used to make electronic components, such as printed circuit boards and connectors. These components are then used to make calculators, computers, televisions, and telephones. Gold is used because it conducts electricity well, is malleable, and does not corrode. Gold is also ductile, which means it can be drawn into a thin wire. For example, 1 ounce (28 g) of gold can be stretched into a wire that is 60 miles (97 kilometers) long.

One of the more striking uses of gold is for decoration on the domes and ceilings of some public buildings. These structures are covered with gold leaf, which is made by pounding gold into very thin sheets. The sheets are so thin that you can actually see through them! These thin gold sheets are then carefully applied to a prepared surface.

The gold leaf will long outlast any paint because gold does not corrode.

This is an aerial view of a synchrotron, which can make gold particles. The synchrotron is the round structure and measures 4 miles (6 km) around.

Imagine if people long ago knew how many different ways gold could be used. They may have tried even harder to turn lead into gold.

Today, scientists know that this can be done. A huge device known as a synchrotron is needed to turn lead into gold. A synchrotron costs many millions of dollars. As a result, the cost of turning lead into gold is far greater than the gold's worth.

Fun Facts About Gold

- In 1854, a California prospector discovered a chunk of gold that weighed almost 200 pounds (90 kg).

- The windows of the cockpit of a jet airplane are coated with a very thin layer of gold. This protects the pilots' eyes from the harmful light of the sun's rays.

- The coffin in which King Tutankhamen was buried was made of gold and weighed about 250 pounds (115 kg).

- A touch-tone telephone contains thirty-three parts made of gold.

- About 90 pounds (40 kg) of gold are used in the construc-tion of a space shuttle.

- The largest lump of gold ever found was discovered in Australia in 1872. It weighed more than 600 pounds (280 kg) and contained about 220 pounds (100 kg) of pure gold.

To Find Out More

If you would like to learn more about gold, check out these additional resources.

 **Books**

Angliss, Sarah. **Gold.** Benchmark Books, 2000.

Gibbons, Faye. **Hernando De Soto: A Search for Gold and Glory.** John F. Blair Publishers, 2003.

Kassinger, Ruth. **The Story of Gold.** Millbrook Press, 2003.

Roop, Peter and Connie Roop. **California Gold Rush.** Scholastic Reference, 2002.

Gold
http://pubs.usgs.gov/gip/ prospect1/goldgip.html

Read about the history of gold starting with the ancient Egyptians five thousand years ago. Learn about the difference between "rolled gold plate," "gold flashed," and "gold washed" jewelry. This site also has information on places where gold is mined in the United States.

Basic Facts About Gold
http://www.tomashworth. com/facts.shtml

This site explains the difference between lode gold mined from rocks and placer gold taken from rivers and streams. You can also read about some other properties of gold, such as its melting point, its specific gravity, and ways to dissolve it.

Industrial Uses of Gold
http://www.gold.org/ discover/knowledge/ aboutgold/industrial_uses

The wide variety of uses of gold in industry is covered in this site. Learn how gold helped put men on the moon, is used by dentists, and keeps buildings cool during the summer.

Turning Lead into Gold
http://www.chemistry. about.com/library/weekly/ aa050601a.htm

Lead can be turned into gold. This site explains what must be done in a process known as transmutation. You will discover that scientists can change a number of elements besides lead into different elements.

Important Words

alchemy practice of changing one element into another, such as lead into gold

alloy substance made by mixing a metal with one or more other elements that keep their individual properties

conductor substance through which electricity or heat passes

ductile capable of being drawn into a wire or pressed into a thin sheet

element building block of matter

karat unit used to show the purity of a gold sample

malleable capable of being pounded into various shapes without breaking

matter stuff or material that makes up everything in the universe

Index

Meet the Author

Salvatore Tocci is a science writer who lives in East Hampton, New York, with his wife Patti. He was a high school biology and chemistry teacher for almost thirty years. His books include a high school chemistry textbook and an elementary school series that encourages students to perform experiments to learn about science. Some of the pocket watches he collects have either an 18-karat gold or a gold-filled case.

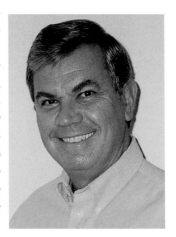

Photographs © 2005: Art Resource, NY/Bildarchiv Preussischer Kulturbesitz: 15; Corbis Images: 43 (James L. Amos), 12 (Craig Aurness), 39 (Morton Beebe), 25 top (Bettmann), 1 (Chris Collins), 36 (Richard Cummins), 31 (Robert Holmes), 7 top (Steve Starr), 40 (Michael S. Yamashita); Dembinsky Photo Assoc./Mark A. Schneider: 27; Photo Researchers, NY/Charles D. Winters: 7 bottom; PhotoEdit: 21 (Robert Brenner), 25 bottom (Jeff Greenberg); The Image Bank/Getty Images/Gianni Cigolini: cover, 2.